Barefoot & Brave

Dr Ifshan Mehraj

Dedication

For the woman I was, who survived.
For the woman I am, who endures.
For the woman I am becoming, who will rise.
And for every woman finding her way—may you walk
barefoot and brave.

Preface

Life has a way of teaching us the most profound lessons through both joy and pain. This collection of poems is a reflection of my journey—through love, heartbreak, motherhood, and self-discovery. Each piece carries a part of my soul, a whisper of emotions I've felt deeply, and truths I've come to embrace.

As a woman, a mother, and a seeker, I have walked through storms and stood in the light. I've experienced the raw ache of broken promises and the quiet strength that emerges from healing. These poems are not just words on paper; they are echoes of my heart's journey— an unfiltered glimpse into the vulnerability, resilience, and courage it takes to love, to let go, and to begin again.

This book is for those who have loved fiercely, lost deeply, and dared to hope again. It's for anyone who has stood at the crossroads of pain and healing, choosing to move forward with grace and strength.

May these words resonate with your heart, offering comfort, understanding, and perhaps a sense that you're not alone. My hope is that, within these pages, you will find a reflection of your own experiences and the strength to embrace your journey with an open heart.

Acknowledgements

First and foremost, I am eternally grateful to **Allah** for His endless mercy and grace. Without His guidance and blessings, I would not have found the strength to walk this path, to heal, and to grow into the woman I am today. Every step of this journey has been guided by His light, and I am humbled by the love and protection I continue to receive.

To my precious son, Amaan—your love is my greatest inspiration. Through your eyes, I've learned what it means to love unconditionally and to embrace life with pure joy. You are the light that guides me, and every word I write carries the warmth of your love.

To my sister—your strength, loyalty, and unshakable support have been my anchor through life's storms. You have been my confidante, my protector, and my biggest cheerleader. This journey would have been impossible without your constant presence by my side.

To my parents—my father, whose tough love taught me resilience, and my mother, whose grace and strength continue to guide me. Your lessons have shaped me into the woman I am today.

To my beloved Naani—your stories, wisdom, and fierce spirit have left an indelible mark on my soul. You live on in every word I write and every choice I make.

To my therapist—your gentle guidance and patience have helped me peel back the layers of pain and rediscover my true self. Thank you for holding space for my healing.

A special thank you to **someone who taught me how to love again**— I want you to know that your presence in my life has shown me that love, in its purest form, is possible again. Your kindness and understanding have been a gift, and I carry that lesson with me always.

And finally, to every reader who picks up this book— thank you for allowing my words to find a place in your heart. May you find comfort, strength, and a reflection of your own journey within these pages.

With all my love and gratitude,

Dr Ifshan Mehraj

1. Path to Self Discovery

In years gone by, I've come to see,
Life's not just love and its decree.
Finding one's path, one's own true call,
Is more than chasing love's enthrall.

Love is sweet, a cherished part,
Yet not the sole beat of the heart.
Beyond the quest for someone's grace,
Lies a journey, your own space.

Discover who you truly are,
What you seek, your guiding star.
Relationships may come and fade,
But with yourself, the bond is made.

Focus on growth, happiness true,
Let your spirit guide you through.
Love will come and find it's place,
But don't let it all be a chase.

A world awaits beyond the fray,
Embrace it fully, seize the day.

2. The Longing Within

The chatter within, a restless song,
A longing so deep, it feels so strong.
To build a life, just me and you,
Is it too much, or do you feel it too?

Your signals sway, like whispers unclear,
A dance of doubt I hold so near.
I love you still, with all my heart,
Yet wonder—are we worlds apart?

This yearning grows, it takes its toll,
On fragile dreams and my aching soul.
Each day I crave to hold you tight,
To pour my heart, to make it right.

To talk, to laugh, to soothe your pain,
To stand with you through joy and rain.
I dream of you as my heart takes flight,
To chase the shadows, to bring you light.

So tell me, love, do you feel the same?
Or am I alone in this tender flame?

3. Guarding Peace

In a world of noise and ceaseless strife,
Find your inner peace and hold it tight.
Chaos reigns and distractions call,
Yet sacred calm can conquer all.

It's the eye within the storm's fierce might,
The quiet hush in darkest night.
Fight for peace, your precious gem,
Guard it like a diadem.

Steal moments solely for your soul,
Set boundaries firm to keep you whole.
Say no to things that drain your fire,
Tune out the world's unending choir.

Peace isn't given, it's dearly earned,
Through choices made and lessons learned.
Once you grasp it, never let go,
Your anchor strong in life's wild flow.

4. The Wounds I Carried

I hid my wounds beneath my skin,
Ignoring pain that pulsed within.
I pushed ahead with silent cries,
Afraid to let the hurt arise.

I wore my strength like fragile steel,
Pretending scars would never feel.
With tired steps and heavy heart,
I ran from healing's tender start.

I turned my face from morning light,
Refusing comfort, warmth, or flight.
But shadows grew, and so did pain,
Each wound unhealed, a deeper stain.

Till one day, broken, I could see—
The strength I lost was all of me.
To heal, I knew I had to bend,
To feel the hurt, to let it mend.

So I embraced each scar and tear,
Uncovered wounds and faced them there.
And gently, slowly, I became,
A soul reborn from soot and flame.

5. A Brave Beginning

Divorce is not the fall we fear,
But courage speaking, loud and clear.
A step away from chains that bind,
A journey toward the self we find.

In broken vows, a voice takes flight,
In darkest days, we find the light.
Toxic ties, we leave behind,
To heal the soul, to free the mind.

Through tears we walk, through fear we stand,
Reclaiming life with steady hand.
We break the mold, we rise anew,
Rediscovering what's pure and true.

With every ending, hope takes wing,
A future bright with songs to sing.
This is not loss, nor love's defeat,
But the path where courage and freedom meet.

6. Unfinished and True

We are messy, incomplete, undone,
Carrying shadows, yet facing the sun.
Bruised by life, yet learning to stand,
Soft, raw, and human, hand in hand.

We don't know it all, we never will,
Our hearts tremble, our voices spill.
Admitting mistakes, breaking apart,
Revealing the chaos that lives in our heart.

We cry, we shake, we dare to say,
The truths we've hidden, the fears we delay.
No longer perfect, no need to pretend,
Just humans, unguarded, beginning to mend.

And in this mess, we find our place,
A deeper love, a tender grace.
Nothing to prove, nothing to defend,
Only connection, where walls end.

We are unfinished, but beautifully so,
Growing together, letting it show.

7. Discomfort: A Hidden Teacher

Discomfort.
We all try to escape it.
It feels too heavy, too sharp, too overwhelming.
But what if it's not here to harm you?
What if it's here to guide you?
Take a moment.
Stop running.
Feel the unease.
Let it exist.
It's not easy—I know.
But this is where growth begins.
The pain that weighs you down,
The fear that holds you back,
The uncertainty that clouds your mind—
They're not here to punish you.
They're here to teach you.
What lesson lies beneath the struggle?
What truth is waiting to be uncovered?
Don't turn away.

Stay with it.
One day, you'll realize:
The discomfort you feared
Was the path to your strength.

8. The Call of the Soul

Sometimes, I feel it deep inside,
A pull I can't explain or hide.
It's not about success or fame,
Or anyone knowing my name.

I just want to be who I am,
No masks, no lies, no hidden plan.
To stand in my truth, messy and real,
To show the world how I really feel.

I want to be seen, to let it all out,
To know who I am, without a doubt.
This is the call I can't ignore—
To be myself, nothing more.

9. Embracing My Journey

In the tapestry of my life, traumas woven, Yet from their threads, strength is hewn. I've trod the path, filled with breadcrumbs thin, Now, I seek to love myself, from within.

A mother's love, pure and bright, Through Amaan's eyes, a guiding light. Unconditional, his love does flow, Teaching me what I didn't know.

Healing scars, both seen and unseen, A journey ongoing, yet serene. With each step forward, I am shown, The woman within, steadily grown.

My sister, a pillar, steadfast and true, Guiding me when I didn't know what to do. My father's love, sometimes tough, Yet lessons learned, enough's enough.

My mother, embodiment of strength and grace, Her resilience, a guiding embrace. Naani dear, a force to behold, Her legacy, in stories untold.

And in the therapist's gentle care, Learning to accept, to repair. Childhood's wounds, now understood, Accepting myself, as I should.

So, I embrace this journey, wild and free, For it has shaped the woman in me. With gratitude, I tread each day, For in this journey, I find my way.

10. The Quiet Symphony

Love speaks softly,
not in grand gestures or sweeping words,
but in making someone feel seen,
truly heard, deeply understood.

It's a hand held gently,
an attentive gaze,
the kind of listening that goes beyond words.
A moment where the world fades,
and all that's left is the one before you.

It's knowing their heart's hidden language,
offering a space without judgement,
a shelter for their unspoken storms.

Seeing the world as they do,
walking paths you may never tread,
yet still holding them close.

In this silent symphony,

a love so loud:
"I see you. I hear you. I understand you.
And you are loved.

11. The Lesson of Boundaries

What you allow, you choose to repeat,
A pattern laid beneath your feet.
No line drawn, no boundary clear,
Invites the harm you silently fear.

By saying yes when you mean no,
You teach the world the seeds to sow.
And every time you compromise,
You trade your truth for fleeting lies.

It's not just firmness, but self-respect,
A lesson we often neglect.
To honor your heart, to guard your peace,
Let courage in, and fear release.

So draw the line, stand firm, be kind,
Respect yourself—your heart, your mind.
For every boundary you create,
Shapes a life that's truly great.

12. Awakening

I stopped reaching for the sky
And found my truth where I stand.
For years, I thought freedom meant
Escaping pain, leaving it behind.

But I was wrong.

Awakening lives in the mess of life—
In heartbreak, struggles, and quiet moments.
Grief opened me, anger gave me fire,
And joy stretched my heart wide.

True freedom isn't rising above;
It's standing firm, feeling it all.
Not running, not hiding, just living—
Alive, grounded, and whole

13. What If We Really Lived?

How far we drift from this moment,
Not the busy, ticking clock moment,
But the raw, sacred breath of now,
Where we tremble, deeply feeling,
Where life reveals its fragile face.

I've seen souls awaken at the edge,
On death beds, whispering truths,
Eyes wide with love they never spoke,
Grasping at last what their hearts held,
Too late to live it in the world's rush.

If only they'd reached sooner,
What would they have become,
Alive to love, to grief, to joy?
Would they have burned too bright,
Or found a way to hold it all?

What must we break, or heal,

To let hearts lead the dance,
To live, laugh, and love so deeply
That even in life's harsh storm,
Our souls still breathe this moment?

14. The Warmth Within

I searched for love in every space,
In every bond, each sweet embrace,
In wins, in losses, high and low,
In every place I dared to go.

I tried to fill the hollow ache,
With all but what my heart would take:
A touch, so soft, from my own hand,
The gentleness I'd longed to land.

It's strange, the way we run and hide,
From what could heal us deep inside.
We think we're flawed, too worn to mend,
To give ourselves the love we send.

But now I learn to stay, to wait,
To hold myself through doubt and weight,
To be the one I'd often flee,
To feel, in that, the warmth of me.

15. Knowing When to Walk Away

They asked me why I let them go,
why I don't reach out, don't say hello.
I gave the truth, simple and clear,
but they replied, "Be bigger, my dear."

But being "bigger" isn't the way
if it means reliving yesterday.
Some wounds don't heal by holding on,
some ties are meant to come undone.

I tried, I gave, I did my part,
but peace is worth more than a heavy heart.
So I choose silence, I choose release,
I choose myself, I choose my peace.

16. Seen with the Heart

In the end, I've come to see,
We don't need to change to be worthy, to be free.
All our days, we strive and bend,
Trying to be prettier, wiser in the end.

But I've learned two things, soft and true—
The ones who love us, see through and through.
With hearts wide open, they'll always find,
Qualities in us that we may leave behind.

And those who choose not to let love in,
Will stay untouched by all we've given.
Their eyes unsatisfied, their vision blind,
No effort we make will change their mind.

So here I stand, my flaws on display,
No more polishing them away.
For those who see me, faults and all,
Are the ones who'll catch me when I fall.

Our imperfections, left as they are,
Become a mirror of who sees with the heart.

17. The Love That Was Always Mine

I thought I loved like never before,
A love so vast, it shook my core.
"I'll never feel this way again,"
I whispered through the ache and pain.

But then the truth began to gleam,
A quiet light, a softened beam.
The love I gave, so pure, so true,
Was not from them—it came from you.

It wasn't theirs, that sacred flame,
They were but mirrors in love's name.
A place to pour what always burned,
A lesson in love's depth I learned.

The heart that loved, it still beats strong,
The song it sings, it still belongs.
To me, the lover, ever whole,
With love that radiates from my soul.

So when they're gone, I'll still remain,
The love within, untouched by pain.
It's mine to give, to hold, to shine—
This love was always, ever mine.

18. The Weight of Love

Everyone has tasted the sting of pain,
Left fingerprints on hearts, left bruises and stains.
Each soul who's dared to be held or to hold,
Has traded dreams for moments warm yet cold.

Everyone walks with a shadow of shame,
Moments tucked away, but all just the same.
No soul exempt, no heart untouched,
Time bears witness to the scars and such.

Every second, each choice, comes with a toll—
Doors opened wide, others closed to the soul.
The memories we keep, and those we must lose,
The love that we seek, and the love we bruise.

Love, we think, is a flawless dream,
Perfect and bright, an endless stream.
But love is only as pure as we,
Bound by flesh, flawed as we can be.

And when they say, "If it hurts, it's not true,"
I wonder what life they've been living through.
For love that's real is joy and ache,
The sweetest risk we ever take.

So, if love brought you pain, fear not its name,
For pain is part of this tender game.
It wasn't life, if it didn't burn—
And love isn't love, if no lessons are learned.

19. Unspoken Refrain

Here I write this again, with a heart full of pain,
Unspoken words, like an endless refrain.
You have no time for me, it cuts deep inside,
No efforts, no planning, no space by your side.

Stuck in your work, with balance unkept,
I wait in the shadows, my heart has wept.
A thing in your life, dusted off when you please,
Where am I in this? My soul seeks release.

What of my needs, the time I've implored,
Moments to share, conversations adored?
Isn't it bare minimum, to sit and to plan?
To love and to cherish, as best as you can?

Still I choose love, despite the neglect,
Hoping one day, you'll see and reflect.
I fear growing used to the absence, the ache,
For when I'm gone, your heart too may break.

Value me now, before it's too late,
Love me, cherish me, before sealing our fate.

20. Shattered Echoes

A part of me broke,
Again and again, I shattered,
When you said you had no needs,
And never checked if I mattered.

You spoke of time, the hour too late,
A hollow silence, words withheld.
You told me, "Leave me, decide alone,"
And with each word, my spirit fell.

Your work, unchanging as you claimed,
Why pursue me at all, I wondered.
Now a single sorry drips from lips,
But the hurt still thunders.

You seem fine, so unaware,
Of all the pain you left behind.
I gave my all, my pride, my self,
Yet to your needs, I was blind.

I adjusted, accepted, stood by you,
Ready to support, to make things right,
But you, indifferent, distant, cold,
Held me only when it fit your sight.

I begged for the barest warmth,
For crumbs that never came,
I loved you with an open heart,
And all you gave was pain.

21. Sadly, That Won't Last Long

He says the words you crave to hear,
Whispers promises in your ear.
Knows all the faults your heart laments,
Crafts his love to your discontent.

He plays the role of perfect man,
Corrects the flaws your lover can.
A mission now, his only aim—
To steal your heart, to win this game.

But pause and see the fleeting chase,
His love is not a lasting place.
There's a difference, don't mistake,
Between pursuit and love that's fake.

For men can spend on fleeting lust,
Do all they must, betray your trust.
A hunter's drive, his goal in sight,
Can blind you with a borrowed light.

So don't be fooled by fleeting charm,
Protect your love, keep safe from harm.
Help the one who's truly yours,
Build a bond that time ensures.

For love is forged, not simply found,
In roots that grow beneath the ground.
Teach your love the ways you crave,
And make your bond a love to save.

22. Crumbs and Cake

I've waited in shadows, in hopes and in dreams,
Craving your presence, or so it seems.
Yearning for moments, a glimpse of your face,
But all that I'm given feels like a chase.

You say that you're fine, that life's just a race,
Yet, I'm left here wondering, lost in this space.
Crumbs of affection, just slivers of light,
When I asked for the cake, the fullness, the right.

I wanted your time, just the basics and care,
A balance of love, something we could share.
But all that I hear is how different life's been,
As if my needs are just dust in the wind.

It hurts, this silence, the lack of your sight,
As if I'm not worth a moment, a night.
Everything else seems to take up your mind,
And here I am, waiting, feeling left behind.

Don't settle for crumbs when you deserve the whole
cake,
I whisper to myself, for my own sake.
Yet, here I remain, torn between love and despair,
Wondering if you even care.

Am I just not important, not part of your plan?
Is it too much to ask to feel loved by a man?
These thoughts weigh heavy, they tear me apart,
For all I had wanted was a place in your heart.

23. The Echo of Silence

My silence speaks of battles done,
No longer fighting, nothing to be won.
It tells of weary hearts and tired pleas,
Of feelings explained, now lost in the breeze.

My silence whispers of changes embraced,
No longer longing, no complaints traced.
It's the quiet of a soul seeking peace,
A healing journey, where old desires cease.

My silence holds the grace of letting go,
With dignity, I move, as rivers flow.
No words left to share, no wishes to renew,
Just silence, as I gracefully forget you.

24. The Day I Stopped Fighting Small Fights

I stopped fighting those who whispered lies,
Their voices small, like fading cries.
I stopped the battles with those near,
In-laws' judgment, once so clear.

I stopped the war for fleeting fame,
No need for praise, no need for name.
I stopped the chase for what they'd see,
Public dreams that weren't for me.

I stopped defending against the fools,
Their petty games, their senseless rules.
I let them fight, I walked away,
To find my own, a brighter day.

And in that silence, dreams took flight,
I fought for vision, chased the light.
My purpose strong, my soul alive,
In destiny, I chose to thrive.

The day I gave up on small strife,
Was the day I truly found my life.

Some fights are not worth your time,
Choose what you fight for, wisely.

25. The Right Man's Promise

The wrong man shows you everyday.
You can survive alone, be strong.
He lets you carry all the weight,
As if you have known it all along.
But the right man sees your strength within,
And though he knows what you can do,
He'll never let you walk alone,
He'll stand by you, so true.
Together, hand in hand you will go,
Sharing burdens, hearts aligned.
In unity, your strength will grow.
In partnership, true love you'll find.
A real man sets the tone with care,
Consistent, steady, always true.
He shows up for you, standing there,
Leading with love in all he'll do.
For in his arms, you will find your peace.
A safety born from love so deep.
With him, your worries find release.
In his embrace, you safely sleep.

26. Be the Lighthouse

Don't strive to steer another's course,
Or grasp the helm of a distant dream.
Be the lighthouse, firm and bright,
Guiding with a quiet, gentle gleam.

Stand tall, let your light shine true,
And those adrift will find their way to you.

27. My Safe Space

The best feeling comes with each step I take,
Toward your home, where my soul awakes.
Something about you completes my heart,
A yearning, a craving, we're never apart.

Through each long day, I look forward to you,
Sharing meals, simple talks, dreams old and new.
I love how you tease me, call out my drama,
Moments that fill my world with pure panorama.

The way you touch me, how we just sit,
Together in silence, yet perfectly lit.
There's a peace in doing nothing at all,
A strength you give that makes me stand tall.

Resting my head on your gentle chest,
That safe space where I find my rest.
You're so kind, so gentle, a love so true,
I treasure each moment, every side of you.

I pray our love grows, steady and bright,
That we be each other's joy, each other's light.
Even when we argue, love finds a way,
Choosing you still, each and every day.

You are my cherished, my heart's true desire,
The spark that sets my soul on fire.
Blessed be our love, a never-ending place,
Where I find everything—my heart, my safe space.

28. Whispers of Us: A Love Unveiled

In a park's serene embrace, fate took its gentle hand,
Never did I fathom you'd be so special, so grand.
Friendship's veil adorned our path, yet destiny's decree,
Unveiled a love profound, that set my spirit free.

Your presence, a soothing balm, brought peace anew, In
your eyes, I found solace, a tranquil view. With each
passing moment, my heart found its song, Enraptured by
the melody, that with you, I belong.

From strolling in the park to our very first lunch, Every
moment with you, a treasure, a hallowed bunch. Our
drive to Gurgaon, etched in memory's embrace, Each
shared experience, a . journey, a sacred space.

In the simplicity of moments, lies a love untold, Every
laugh, every smile, a story to behold. From brewing tea
to lying by your side, In serving you, in loving you, my
joy abides.

So let this verse be a testament, my love, To the bond we share, ordained from above. In your arms, I find my truest home, Forever grateful, as we journey, hand in hand, to roam.

29. Gratitude

Each day, let gratitude light our way,
For simple things we often overlook,
The phone we use, the food we eat,
The water flowing from a brook.
A roof above, clothes to wear,
A cupboard filled with life's supply,
Our health intact, our sprits free,
Blessings that money cannot buy.
In struggles seen and unseen too,
We never know what others bear,
So let our hearts be full and true,
With gratitude beyond compare.
For when we fill our lives with thanks,
Abundance flows in every part,
We live our lives more fully then,
With gratefulness within our heart.
So cherish all, both great and small,
From dawn until the day is through,
For in this act of gratitude,
Life's blessings come to you a new.